# Other Concerns & Brother Clark

BY HOLLIS SUMMERS

*Poetry*

Occupant Please Forward
Start from Home
Sit Opposite Each Other
The Peddler and Other Domestic Matters
Seven Occasions
Someone Else
The Walks Near Athens

*Novels*

The Garden
The Day After Sunday
The Weather of February
Brighten the Corner
City Limit

*Short Stories*

How They Chose the Dead
Standing Room

# Other Concerns & Brother Clark

HOLLIS SUMMERS

Ohio University Press    Athens

Ohio University Press books are printed on acid-free paper. ∞

Library of Congress Cataloging-in-Publication Data

Summers, Hollis Spurgeon, 1916-
Other concerns & Brother Clark.

I. Title.  II. Title: Other concerns and Brother Clark.
PS3537.U7208   1988        811'.54        88-19655
ISBN 0-8214-0910-7 (alk. paper)
ISBN 0-8214-0911-5 (pbk. : alk. paper)

*For Daniel, William, Hollis, David*

# Contents

*[III]*

## Acknowledgments

Many of these poems first appeared in *Kentucky Writings,*
*Athens Magazine, Ann Arbor Review, Cornfield Review,*
*University of Windsor Review,* and *Poetry Now.* The long
poem "Brother Clark" first appeared in *The Ohio Review.*
Ohio University Press is grateful to these journals for
their kind permission to reprint these poems in this
volume and regrets any inadvertent omission of
acknowledgment for other poems which may have
been published previously.

# Other Concerns & Brother Clark

*[I]*

## Transfiguration

The air stands still.
The air stands still.
The tree lashes itself,
every heart shaped leaf trembles—

no, shakes, waves.

The tree is only a tree
in anguish—

no, moving.

The tree imagines, pretends—

no, the trunk of the tree
shakes every heart shaped leaf
as if wind happens.
I press my face against a screen;
in still air the tree is

    They still open and close.
    They still open and close,
    those transported Japanese clams,
    on Japanese time.

In San Francisco,
a hundred generations later,
they remember home.

3

Impatient with tradition
times and tides,
I too, recall, recall

the cherry tree.
Of course thunder is a chariot,
machine driven, rounding boulders,
circling the sky of Athens Ohio,
pausing over our house,
to race again, to shout at our house
whose rooftop tries to reach the sky.

Lightning has nothing to do with the chariot.
Chariot wheels flare only small sparks.
Despite what we've been told,
lightning comes from something else;
Somebody chases every chariot.
Today He found our cherry tree.

*We lure each other.*

Still
missing
the presence
of eagles
or prophets,
the chickadees
and we,
at suet
and prayer,
manage
dusk
still.

We lure each other.

## Twelve Gray Gulls

Twelve gray gulls stand like counters in a game
without an opponent,
not moving even when low flying advertising planes
ruffle their feathers;

they do not move to get a better view of anything:
they hold a reasonless pattern;
they make a pattern of nothing.
I may applaud the gulls.

## Hydrangeas

They are too old to live
but they hold at color
as if they lived.
They are older
than the behatted ladies
taking the sun
in the cathedral square
pinching at pieces of sweet
from their identical paper bags.

Some are green and gray,
the color of bones dogs
leave, forgetting where;
they are the pink you remember
when you cannot remember color;
they are blue, tan,
globes of crumpled veins
or paper bags
nodding in the cathedral sun.

*Bijou*

Pedigreed,
almost beyond being,
runt of the litter,
she was born blind
subject to fits of epilepsy;

but somebody wanted her,
we did,
whether from vanity
or charity
I have not determined.

She has adjusted,
total with our exits and entrances
and stairways;
she protects the house
totally.

Her fits are brief,
her affection
marked,
her bark
a kind of music.

We have taken her on long trips.
She admires everywhere,
finding all exits and entrances
and stairways.
She eyes us.

We consider giving her away,
or, more, putting;
her joy
proves a burden
for everyone.

## Semantics

Grief finds no use for consonants
while vowels cry in any language
A, E, O for the moments
when no words assuage
any grief we know.

And joy, too, surges wordless.

Here: you, I, aayeeoo,
For this moment's happiness.

## Heat

The sun pressed its hard hands
flat on his head;
but the earth, frozen with heat,
would not admit him.

The sun hammered harder
and harder and harder again,
and still the earth refused him.

Only poisonous weeds,
nurtured when hands moved gentle
inhabited the earth around him;

he was a nail
no board would admit:
Adam, of course,
entertaining the curse.

## An Afternoon in the Life of

He slept, dreaming of an actor
forgetting his lines in a theater
where his play wasn't playing anyhow;

he was a painter out of paint
working for an audience at a canvas
big as the floor of a wrestling ring;

he was a librarian controlling a billion books
of blank pages, confronted by a queue
of readers waiting beyond infinity;

he wanted to tell everybody
something everybody already knew;
he woke speechless; and slept again;

and woke; telling himself
he dreamed,
knowing he did not dream.

## The Intersection

Granted, I had driven
seven inches over the pedestrian
crossing line,

but not enough to prevent
a street full of humanity
from crossing over and back again,

hardly enough to warrant
the old man's shattering my headlights
with the knob of his cane:

he advanced,
not uttering a word,
to craze the windshield;

he, then, strolled
across the intersection,
smiling.

I drive in the dark world under water.
Perhaps my vision matches the old man's own.
I had wanted to run him down.

## The Spy

From the hill above the playground
I have watched for a month of noons
The winter children play. I have not found
My son for sure in the blurred moons
Of the confetti faces whose wool legs map
A blossom on the jungle gym.
Although I know the color of his cap
I cannot find him.

This hill is tall. Voices sound like a summer
Pool from here. For years
I have known that winter air sieves
Winter eyes and ears.
I am almost sure I do not know the face
Of the figure who scrapes his foot, alone
Against splotched stone, waiting recess.
He is not my son, my son.

## Juan

He died four days after the hospital admitted him.
His body was embalmed and brought back home.
After a wake of three days, we buried him.

My wife dreamed that Juan asked to be exhumed.
He said, "I'm not dead."
He said, "My eyes are filled with mud, Mamma."

He said, "Make Pappa visit my grave."
I attended Juan on All Soul's day, two months after his burial.
I shouted over his grave my love. I employed my shovel.

The glass of the coffin was broken.
Mud, indeed, covered Juan's eyes.
We brought him home. We dressed him in clean clothes.

Juan's face shines pink. His eyes glare.
We can see nerves on the skin of his hands.
His eyelids refuse to close.

My mother believes the fairies have abducted Juan:
she thinks his body is only a carved banana trunk.
My father believes the demons wish to confuse us.

My wife and I face a quandary
The Sanitation Inspector visits us twice a day.
We pray to know how often parents must bury their dead.

## The Confessional Booth

1.

The girl tiptoed past the rest of us
who waited for rain to stop,
past the lighted confessional booth
to sit in a funeral chair and wait her turn
for the fat priest ensconced, enshrined
in the curlecued booth under a light bulb,
his fat chin in his hand,
listening or not listening
to a crippled pale woman
who surely told no sins worth mentioning.

2.

But the priest seemed interested
in what the girl was willing to say
from her kneeling half darkness;
he lowered his hand to smooth his cassock;
perhaps he did not force the girl to cry.

I think the girl cried, "Father."

But any cry in whispered silences
of a foreign cathedral
sounds loud to a hiker
who waits for rain to stop.

3.

I have no specific defense
for my rushing the booth,
for breaking the light with my rucksack;
the priest was only a lady who sells tickets
to a play she has not seen,
a man who waits in a telephone stall
for a call that will not, possibly, come,
a child pretending to sit on a throne.
Having pretended and waited and sold, myself,
I, now, stand in line, ambushing the priest.

## Man Walking

Walking north on a far southern beach
colder than a northern winter's childhood,
remembering the child's ears, hands, feet
he assumed forever frozen
and the sound of his crying,
the bark of a dog caught in barbed wire,

I met a man in a hooded coat,
a ski mask, boots, gloves,
his arm stretched behind him
as if he pulled a heavy object on a leash,
I pretended I did not see him.
Perhaps he did not see me.

His boots have left no marks on the sand,
but I walked another mile before I turned
to walk back home with the wind.
The sand held only the prints
of my northbound feet.
I am not sure I heard the bark of a dog.

## The Flock

You have to throw marbles—
I choose light blue ones,
the color of sky
just after morning,
ten o'clock June sky—
in with the feed
to interest baby turkeys.

The babies peck
at the glittering blue,
unwittingly, take
a beakful of food
by chance,
and grow.

Turkeys' natural habits
do not include eating.
Even after they acquire
an eating habit,
they will refuse to eat
from a strange feeder.

They suffer from high blood pressure,
like mine, or yours.

A child's scream
can panic turkeys,
causing collective
heart attacks.

I do not allow children
to wander my farm,
even in light blue June.
I am opposed to children.
Turkeys, my turkeys,
too fat to mate,
breed artificially

Last year a fire
started by a child
killed seven thousand
of my birds.
State inspection officials
visit my farm almost daily
concerned with specifications
about slaughter.

State men,
like children,
prove rough
on turkey farmers.

Prices are good this year.
They will rise, they will lower.
I write these words as a prophet,
for after
I am dead.

A turkey is
the most stupid animal
in the world.
They serve us right.

20

## Such is the Nature of

Although rarely more than half our size
the puppets assume they act on their own,
considering us only when
the story turns out wrong:
heroes and heroines should get married at the end.

The audience can always leave the theater;
only the puppets and the puppeteers
hang doomed together for the evening,
blaming each other, bound to the hall,
no matter how free they pretend to be.

*Waking*

I dreamed the town,
or I'd been half asleep,
envying the instant sleep of natives
who snored themselves asleep
and out and back again;

I had slung my feet
over the bus seat next to me,
pretending I was native
born in a sudden town square.

    The square lay tan,
    blooming dirty bougainvillea;
    I had dreamed or seen
    a desert bird
    flying its mustard shadow.

    Nothing lived, except a burro's carcass,
    alive with replicas
    of the desert bird
    marrying its shadows.

## Nursing Home

### 1. Porch

Normally the two swings hang
the rocking chairs stand
like pictures of swings and rockers
waiting for a resort convention;

oh, a couple of times I have seen them move,
but barely, no more than a sigh
moves the country newspaper you still hold
after having read it all.

The guests, patients, inmates —
we think of ourselves variously —
rarely venture to the porch even in summer
preferring, perhaps, not to admit we live together

But tonight the porch is wild with March;
the swings swoop, the rockers race,
carnival rides gone beserk
with March;

And all evening we have stood and watched
sharing windows together,
even applauding the revelers
as if we loved each other.

## 2. Fire

Our home
shaped like a collage of old ladies' faces
with dark doubled eyes and slashed mouths
burned;

the smoke seeping from the lidded eyes
rose into curling coiffeurs,
grew,

blossomed
into bouffants such as courtesans wore
inspiring extravagant adjectives from courtiers
once,

burned
from white to gray to flame to black
and out, leaving lintel posts
headless

nursing
nothing, not even an amber
of any kind of ideal fire,
absolute.

## 3. Morning

Five real old ladies taken by their smoky dreams,
perhaps even willing to be taken, without curls
died;

five, their thin hair twisted into plastic curlers,
dawn colored, expecting morning,
escaped,

stood
in a line, like silhouette courtesan dolls
cut out of a newspaper by uncertain hands,
considered

dawn,
considered their slovenly dead neighbors,
the sleepy newspaper men with cameras
snapping;

caught
by morning, trying not to laugh,
the remaining ladies patted their plastic heads
and smiled.

*[II]*

## How to Make a Violin

It all begins with wood.
Now that wood is scarce
even in the highlands of South Tyrol
we must search farther than our fathers
traveled.

Choose the northern side
of the waiting tree;
maple for the back, red spruce for the front;
the northern side knows fewer suns,
stands dense and strong

for having waited, as you have waited.
Dry the wood carefully.
Carve the pieces as carefully
as if you carved your own bones.
You are a sculptor, a surgeon,

you are an apothecary, an alchemist.
Carefully apply your natural materials,
herbs, roots, compounds,
finding the varnishes that give
color, tone, resonance.

Perhaps you are not a musician.
But the violin will develop itself
if someone plays it every day
honoring your craft.
Perhaps your sons will listen.

## Minutes for the Reality Class

Ready? It's time for the reality class.
We, all of us and the nurse,
not having met since yesterday,
the tenth of the month,
here in Room Double A,
must rearrange.

> Have the letters of this room changed?
> What is the number of this day?
> What does the clock say this time?
> Twenty-four hours after yesterday?
> We may speak in various languages,
> Pig Latin, Greek, Portuguese;
> but we must hold class.

Never mind the state of the weather
or our own ridiculous names,
this is only Reality Class;
we do not need to say
I or Now;
we do not need to say we
met each other once.

## Adoption

A duck with first sight says Mother
to the first moving object he beholds,
generally, in fact, his natural mother;
and we compliment the brood,
admiring the nature of nature.

But, on occasion, a duck first sights
a moving bear, and the bear
unnoted for his courtesy
accepts the accepting duck
allowing the bird to accompany him anywhere.
Neither considers the nature of nature.

I am careful now. I will make no jokes
about ducking, about bearing
up or down,
having made unlikely choices of my own.

## How to Take a Long Bus Trip to Her Funeral

No, don't bother to compare
there with other wheres
you were sick in, or lost,
or even satisfied.

Do not consider making
a travel guide, taking
now into some ailing future
where you reread what you see.

Look at the Jesus signs, now;
the candles of a pine tree, now;
a redwinged blackbird's wing.
Later you can mourn or sing.

## Be Nice to People Who Are Moving

Be nice to people who are moving
from one decade into another,
particularly to women
who will be forty,
and men who will be forty,
day after tomorrow,

> or ten, or sixty;
> it is terrible to be
> facing teenhood or the golden
> tarnished years,
> or forever.

In these progressive times
you run vast chances of surgery:
your head on somebody else's body.
How will we sort ourselves out
at The Resurrection?

> Go ahead.

> Be nice to everybody.

## Cave Drawing

Let's get this straight:
the world is a disc;
the sun, a woman;
the moon, a man;
ignore earlier reports.

What has happened
will go on happening;
those mythical persons died.
Look at their totems,
rocks, trees, mountains

the sun shines on,
and the moon,
wearing their wounded marks.
Children choose their parents;
they enter the sun to be born.

The moon frowns, appears,
and disappears.
Death is also magic.
Celebrate the chambered nautilus,
a skeleton of the sun, or the moon.

## Why More Men Don't Play Harps

"You expect a woman harpist";
no less than a woman harpist told me,
"men must play infinitely better
to get engagements." She is my therapist.

I turned to the violin;
many men have mastered violins.

But violins like harps
resembled meaning water, dappled ponds,
and remembering something
you thought you'd forgot.

I'm considering tympani,
landed, unwilling to forget.

## Poison Ivy, Jewel Weed

They often grow together,
poison ivy, jewel weed.

The ivy is an erect shrub
or a trailing vine;
generally it climbs;
it climbs whenever it can.
It flourishes in disturbed woods,
not in original forests;
it flourishes most luxuriant
in your own garden.

Your tethered dog, wandering the ivy
trying to stretch your limited garden,
can poison you. Your jolly campfire,
nurtured by ivy, can poison.

But the fables of ivy are not true.
Mere looking will not poison you.
It is no more lethal by night than day.
It does not conjure Satan in a bouquet.

Meanwhile dwells the jewel weed,
its yellow flower a dangling earring,
a pendant for a woman's breasts,
moving as ivy moves in air.

The jewel's succulent stems
will cure your dermatosis.
It will almost always cure.
The family name is touch-me-not.

But it does not mean its name.
Touch the mature plant. The pods pop,
ejecting seeds to grow again
beside our poisonous ivy.

If you choose to poison, poison carefully.
Pain and its cure often grow together.

## Light and Even Lighter

Butterflies fly in the day time
not needing to eat;
having stored food as larvae
they drink nectar;
their useful activity is called
cross pollination.

Defenseless victims
they depend on camouflage.
Part of their color
requires no pigment at all;
light passes through surfaces,
breaks into wave lengths

we call color.
Blue is the structural color,
and iridescent.
You can use them to decorate
serving trays and wastebaskets.
You can mount butterflies.

## How to Determine Origins

First,
the heart pulsing;
then the eyes,
then, feet and wings.

You have to go somewhere
for sustenance,
so you peck
out of the shell,

and there you are.
Here you are
here
first.

# Arlington

All
Day
I
Have Walked
About
Arlington
I
Have Seen
not
Careful          one
We Must          wet
Guard            eye
Against          nor
Our              heard
Inclination      one          Rest in peace
for              cry          is sufficient
Perpetual        about             is
Monuments        Arlington    rest in peace

## Response for an Anniversary

Thank you, but no, please no.
We are not hysterical,
thank you, but, please, no.
Give us no digital watches.

A digital watch
considers only now,
does not allow
a catch in the throat,
memory or hope,
a while ago
or what will happen
this afternoon.

However fine is now,
now does not exist.
Allow us watches that vow
then, after; before, later.

## Notes for a Coffin Lid

You should have learned to accept
Praise as well as blame
Admitting all illogics.

[III]

*Brother Clark*

1.

The boy's parents and Brother Clark
stood by the boy's bed in the glassed side porch,
talking of coal strikes and the weather;
it was time for Brother Clark to leave.

"Will you lead us in a word of prayer, Brother Clark?"

The boy's mother shook her head.
Brother Clark was noted for his long prayers;
his benedictions at church could last almost forever.

"A word," his father said.

"Yes. Yes, Amen." Brother Clark fell to his knees;
the boy's father kneeled on one knee beside the bed;
his mother, shivering, lowered herself into the wicker chair.
The old man began with "Amen" again.

2.

The child was accustomed to prayer,
blessed meals, blessed mornings and nights.
He had visited the sick with his father;
"Shall we have a word of prayer?"
His father asked and prayed,
bringing God and Jesus himself

into rooms filled with starch and flowers,
into little back rooms with lowered shades
smelling of kerosene, urine, salve.

Briefly his father blessed everyone;
prayer was his father's business,
but he did not act as if he owned prayer.

    3.

Brother Clark was thankful for Thanksgiving,
for the time of harvest, for all the world,
for the boy's father, "our new Shepherd Thou hast sent."

The old man's breath puffed into the biting air.

The porch held five wide windows and five wide sills,
a glass door leading to a lawn
where dahlias and lilies had grown for a while
and would grow again, perhaps, and die and grow,
logy with custom, until another family
called the spacious parsonage *home.*

"Preachers' families don't belong to anywhere," his mother often said.

"For these, oh God, yes, Jesus, we give Thee thanks."

4.

The boy snatched glimpses of his own breath
and his own new wrist watch,
a reward for having been a patient patient;
and he looked, in spite of himself, at Brother Clark's face,
the man's right cheek like, surely, no cheek on the face of the earth,
eaten yellow and purple with cancer.

The boy squinched his eyes tight
into moons and rainbows and glanced again.

The time was twenty minutes after ten,
Monday, late November, the newspapers had said so
with pictures of Indians and Pilgrims.

Perhaps, while Brother Clark slept, rats gnawed his face.

5.

That Monday was supposed to be a good day,
the boy's stars said so.
He read "Your Stars" before he read the Funnies;
he was to be lucky in love and get good news;
maybe the girl named Claire would come
to stand outside his windows;
maybe Dr. Glass would call to say,
"Tell that boy, get out of bed";
maybe Dr. Glass had read the wrong x-rays:
the pictures of a spotted lung belonging to an old man
who had already died and left his money to the church.

Brother Clark wept.

6.

Spots on lungs were popular that September.
Before their new shoes were barely scuffed,
before they lost their pencil boxes,
Dr. Glass had sent home to their beds
four members of Miss Hattie's room.

Rest and eggs and air would cure their spots.

Smart Dr. Glass was right;
Malcolm was back to school in two weeks,
Jesse in three, Claire in four.

Five times in bright October Claire visited the boy's windows,
her hair brighter than the birch leaves.

"You get well soon, you hear?" Claire called.

7.

Brother Clark had taken seven minutes from the new watch.

"Oh, praise Thee, God, oh blessed Jesus,
our Savior Who takest away the sins of the world."

His tears glided down the good cheek,
fell slowly among the hills of his sick cheek
to mix with the spit at the corners of his lips.

The parents had bought the watch on time.
Jewel, the cook, told the boy.
He didn't know what *on time* meant.
"But it's mine, isn't it? It's mine?"
"I reckon. Anyhow for a while."

Jewel appeared at the kitchen door, her eyes closed, hugging herself.

8.

Jewel was gravy colored, the color of Brother Clark's lips.

The boy wished she had gone to her room in the basement.

He had seen enough of Jewel these long days,
after the early visitors disappeared,
after his parents began to visit other sick.

The first visitors stood in the front hall, shouting,
"You're on our prayer list. Get well soon!"

He liked to think of their prayers rising all over town,
smoking up the sky. He was not sure Jewel prayed for him.
Jewel was Methodist and almost as tall as the kitchen door.

"Jewel Green, tall as a crane," he told himself.

Jewel liked to say, "Hell is a long time burning."

9.

Jewel did not approve of Baptists.
Every day she stretched the porch into a map of Hell.

"We think we headin the same place," she said,
leaning against the frame of the kitchen door.
But you don't get to Looaville by headin for Nashville."

"Heaven isn't Louisville, Jewel. I've been there."

"There's just one road to Looaville. It ain't necessarily Baptist,
and I ain't time for foolin with you."

"I don't want you to." Jewel disappeared
to shake the kitchen range to flames,
singing dark songs about death and the River Jordan.

He worried about the road to Louisville.

10.

But being sick was not too bad.
He didn't have to dress, fighting long underwear;
he didn't have to go to church and worry over his father's sermons,
or the Wednesday suppers where people chewed at Jello and macaroni;
except for missing the girl named Claire
he didn't mind missing the school where boys in Rest Rooms,
easy with their bodies, laughed and said, "You're the new preacher's kid."

He drew and read. He even knitted at a scarf;
Jewel and his parents promised not to tell. "Promise. Cross your hearts."

He grew fat, outgrowing two sets of flannel pajamas.

"Nogs without the nog will make you well," his mother said.

He told himself secrets about his growing body.

11.
Gardens of Get-Well cards jostled the window sills.

He lay under five covers: he often named the covers,
a blanket from Nova Scotia, a quilt of Dresden plates, a spread of...

"Dead, dead, dead," Brother Clark said.

"I have confessed." Brother Clark was telling on himself.
"I have confessed the cause of my cancer,
the lusts of my flesh, my rotting soul.
I have repented and Thou hast cured."
The old man rocked on his creaking knees.
"And she has been taken and I am left,
dear Jesus, continue forgiveness."

The mother almost stood; the father frowned her down.

12.
The boy floated in the crying of Brother Clark's voice.

He moved his hands under the covers; a knitting needle jabbed his groin.

Brother Clark was making up songs:
"Have Thine Own way, Lord, cleft for me;
Thou are The Potter; let me hide myself in Thee,"
as the boy had made up songs,
"Oh, I am lucky to live in Kentucky,
to live on a porch that sees birch trees."

"God, Jesus, merciful Jesus, God."

The mother gripped her chair arms.
Her hands looked made of wicker.

"Amen," his father said, as if to prove he listened.

13.

An ostrich feather of sun lay on the linoleum floor.
His wrist watch was a picture cut from a catalogue.

No, the watch ran. It was a real watch.

It said a minute more, another minute.

Todd, Mrs. Roland's colored man who lived in the basement next door,
crossed the yard, waving.

Todd was friendly. He always waved. He wore his white jacket.

It was Mrs. Roland's bridge day, the fourth Monday.

The boy lifted his hand.
He hoped Todd knew he was waving.

Over Todd's head a cardinal cut the sky in two.

The boy hoped Mrs. Roland wasn't hearing Brother Clark.

14.

Mrs. Roland was Episcopalian, and her hair was bobbed;
she not only played bridge, she smoked behind her thin curtains;
often she gave parties where men and women moved in the rose parlor,
taking silver glasses from Todd's silver tray;
sometimes the couples danced to fast music,
their laughter louder than the gramophone.

"Were you able to sleep last night?" Jewel and his father asked.

"I didn't hear anything. I didn't."

He could not admit he had pressed his face against the cold glass,
cupping his ears to the laughing music
until all of Mrs. Roland's house turned dark.

"Don't fret. She's not of our faith," his mother told his father.

15.

The boy imagined a sunny hall connecting the two houses.
He imagined Mrs. Roland, who smelled like roses, as his daily friend,
and Todd to talk to, and music wandering through the houses.

"Jewel, you ought to marry Todd and live in both our houses."

"Shame on you, shame!" Her hands were long fists.
"He's trash. Don't never talk that way again."

She slammed the kitchen door to disappear, but not for long.

"You listen to me, boy. You listenin?"

"What's trash, Jewel? Todd's not trash."

"Trash is Todd. And you too, maybe, if you ain't careful."

She began to talk about the road to Louisville again.

Brother Clark was talking about the boy. He was telling God on him.

16.

"Forgive this child his sin, oh Lord,
this child who suffers on his bed of pain;
Thou knowest, only Thou,
the nature of his sin;
if it be Thy will, dear God, forgive,

as Thou hast forgiven me;
and shouldst it be against Thy will, oh God Almighty,
assure him his redemption;
deliver him from eternal Hell,
we pray in the name of Thy only begotten Son,
blessed God, sweet Jesus, deliver him, we pray."

Flames licked the corners of the porch.

17.

What the boy knew of death lay in another town
hidden in his mind with the word *forever*,
some goldfish, a neighbor's dog he was frightened of,
empty seats in church where old ladies once sat,
Mr. Gaines, the milkman who had stopped delivering:
"He's dead," they said, as if he had moved to another route;

and flowers, of course, from daffodils to asters and chrysanthemums.
"They'll come again. Wait," they said of the flowers.
"Mr. Gaines?" "We won't be seeing him again."

"Forever?"

He had cried over the word *forever*.

He hid the word, pretending to be comforted.

18.

"We beseech, we implore Thee," Brother Clark shouted.
"Forgive and forgive. Amen and amen."

The boy did not open his eyes to the movement around him.
the wicker chair, the whispers of his mother's skirt,
the sound of bones rearranging themselves.

Once, a long time ago, he had lain in tall grass
listening to the earth and beneath the earth,
imagining the cries of the eternally damned below.

He had never told anyone about his listening.

He would never tell anyone:
again, now, here, he heard crying forever.

The boy's mother called his name; three times she called.

19.

The watch said, "Brother Clark prayed for fifty-seven minutes."
Both sides of the old man's face smiled.
"Bless you, Son." The old man held the boy's hands.
Jewel had disappeared. Todd crossed the yard again.
"Goodbye, Brother Clark." The boy's mother sounded like sleet.
"Goodbye. Goodbye," the men told each other.
A window closed in Mrs. Roland's parlor.
Brother Clark turned and waved from under the birch trees.

"Time to take your temperature," the father said.
His mother made her usual joke, "And then a nog without the nog."
The boy laughed at the joke.

He tried to think about a word like *nog* which didn't mean.

20.

The mother smiled, shaking the thermometer over the bed.
"How much?" he asked, as he always asked.
"Up a little, only a little. It's the time of day."

The father was smiling, too. "You rest now. You rest for a while."

"That's all I do is rest."

"You're getting well. You're better all the time," the woman said.
The man said, "You're our boy, our fine big boy."

"I don't hurt anywhere. I'm not on any bed of pain."

"Of course you aren't." "You don't," they said.

"I'm sorry for what I did was wrong."

The woman moved to the glass door; the man coughed.
The boy was surprised at the sound of his own crying.

21.

"I couldn't stand it if I go to Hell."

"You believe. You believe on the Lord Jesus Christ?"
His father could have been standing behind a pulpit.
"We know that we have been saved because . . . Whosoever will . . ."

"Tell me I'm on the right road. Tell me I'm saved."

He was being prayed over again.
The boy held to his father's thin shoulders.

His mother said, "Amen." She was straightening the five covers.
"You're saved. You'll go to Heaven.
We'll all go to Heaven together, forever."

The boy's parents looked at each other as if they had just met.

"Now, we'll not talk about it any more," his mother said.

22.

They did not talk about it any more.

Occasionally, his father asked, "You're all right now?
You're not worried about anything, are you, any more?"
His mother put her arms around him, "You're fine?"

"I'm fine. Just look how fine I am."

He was back in school by April,
wearing clothes three sizes larger than September's clothes.
"Bought on time," Jewel told him, but he didn't worry much,
except sometimes: when the girl named Claire called him Fatso Fats;
sometimes at night, though he slept now in a room upstairs;
sometimes when he stood alone on the side porch, whistling.

"Clean as a whistle," Dr. Glass said. "Stay out of that bed."

23.

He was well enough to go to Brother Clark's funeral.

Brother Clark died at fifty-seven, just before Easter.

"He lived as many years as he prayed minutes over me."

"The very idea!" His mother laughed until tears
stood in her eyes, as if she were not remembering.
"But funerals are not for children. You aren't to go."

"I think I should. He called me *Son*"

The boy's mother turned her head.

The service at the church lasted for twenty minutes;
at the graveside, ten; only thirty people attended.

The boy's father conducted the comforting ceremonies.

Everybody said it was very cold for Easter.

24.

It is hard to know how old I was or am.
Sixty is six times ten.
Twelve goes into sixty.
The tables add and multiply,
divide, subtract.
For years Brother Clark has known
all there is to know of nothing,
Heaven or Hell,
my parents, Mrs. Roland, Todd, Claire,
the others.
Older now than Brother Clark ever became

I wait for his prayer to end.

God, blessed Jesus, Lord, have mercy upon us.

## On Requesting a Third Pillow

Maybe it's a matter of breathing better,
maybe it's remembering a painful womb,
maybe it's wanting to be already all ready
half way up, to forget the dreams

    where all the people who finally matter
    conjugate, wearing gauze dominoes,
    rarely concealing who they were or are,
    fooling nobody who dreams.

Yes, thank you. I need a third pillow.
I will wake wearing my own domino
Dominus vobiscum means.
The Lord be with you. Lord, protect our dreams.

*George M. Pullman (1831-1897)*

Pullmans, the Pullman, a compartment in The Pullman.
That's what we used to say
when a trip from Louisville to Pittsburgh
meant a trip around the world
and Pullman meant a name, precise
as Love or God or Sunday Evening.

Nobody travels in a Pullman any more.

Still, this static Sunday Evening
having made love with somebody from around the world
while considering Compartments and God, here
I inhabit a stationary Pullman Compartment
we, whoever we were, perhaps even a family,
once inhabited

and I, perhaps, can never leave:

the car, at least this room,
stands equipped with a moving mechanism
for right and left and up and down and every tangent,
a sound track, a roll of scenery

the Trinity turned to Very High,
all happening behind a careful square of window.

Many artists collaborated to make this ugly scenery:

a single artist would have chanced upon a few good lines;
but the piano roll of environment
painted in water colors with many brushes
first dipped into black
records gray mountains, an ochre plain,
a clutter of scraggling bushes,

the Mountains, the Plain, the Bushes again:

but I tend to forget where I got on;
depending on where I got on
the mountains are downtown buildings,
the plain, dark suburbs,
the bushes, families;
I have traveled enough to name repeating sceneries.

I make no play with your name, George M. Pullman:

the sound track calls
thronged sandals walking beneath a fat woman
a machine typing itself
a harsh toothbrush against a partial plate
a blackboard scratched by dozens of fingernails
slow music played at a vast speed

While I fall and shift and rise and fall again:

where did I get on
to be born in a Pullman compartment
questioning points of vision?
Someone could come
to turn this seat into a moving bed
capable of sleep.

Perhaps this bed could move, George Pullman.

## Getting Back

Accustomed to home
and its categories
I suppose
the shock of redbud
among palm trees
embarrassed me

until here on our hill
a dogwood flowers
among the dark pines
sudden as a secret
I had not known
I needed to know again.